IMPACT OF PANDEMIC

SHWETA BAKSHI

Contents

Acknowledgements

Pandemic impacted millions of lives across the globe and challenged our abilities to run everyday life. While overcoming the challenges, an opportunity for self introspection was created which prompted several Professionals to invent the new ways of living, keeping in pace with the challenges thwart upon them.

As I was also a part of this change, I could vividly see an author within me which embarked me on a journey where as a Professional I could explore opportunities of growth. Although it's my first book and through this book I tried to add considerable facts about technological advancements facilitated several Professionals in reviving their jobs and careers amidst crisis, e-learning platforms kept the learning intact, challenges of online education and learning outcomes.

A great respect for teachers and educators for being patient and raising the education bar high for children via virtual platform. Thisbook is also dedicated to corona warriors who sacrificed their lives to save humanity.

I would like to express gratitude to my elders and family for their support in completing this book. Groveling thanks to educators for bringing significant changes in education and aspiring several to thrive amidst crisis.

Author's Note

A Master's degree in Business Administration and over ten years of experience in various HR domains like Talent Acquisition & Operations, employee engagement. Her passion to learn new skills embarked her on a journey of an author where she used her writing skills to explain the IMPACT OF PANDEMIC.

As she climbed up the corporate ladder, she was able to gain ample knowledge about IT Industry and varied technological advancements with passing years of her Professional experience. She has used sometechnical terms to explain the impact of pandemic on digitalization and subsequently on other industries.

Her keen interest to learn Agile HRM which is a growing interest of several HR Professionals and substantial for sustainable growth of organizations.

CHAPTER I

Impact on our lives

Pandemic which engulfed several lives and entire community succumbed to unprecedented crisis which affected global public health. Life threatening disease caused destruction and enormously impacted our lives. It caused a massive damage to the economy and affected lives of today's generation who were at the crucial stages of life development. Health, education, employment opportunities, income and well being - substantial decline in human development.

To control the spread of corona virus, Government took appropriate measures and billions of people have been asked to stay at home. A nationwide lockdown in the country limited the movement of entire population to control the disease from spreading which caused a sense of fear and uncertainty. Government left no stone unturned and took corrective measures to control the damage.

Though some still had to leave their homes and work despite of restrictions imposed by Government which not only put their lives in risk but their families too. Our community helpers worked day and night to fight against corona virus. Our medical specialist, doctors, nurses, physicians, patient care technicians, police and health care workers who were more prone to corona virus, relentlessly worked to save human lives. The least we can do for them is respect and salute them for their sincere efforts.

Nationwide lockdown restricted economic activities and Public gatherings were banned, travel restrictions were imposed and events cancellations to slow down the effect of coronavirus. Several enterprises, business services, non-essential sectors were closed, tremendously affected employment of several professionals. However, Pandemic affected every Industry across the globe but worst impacted were airlines, tourism, retail, automobile and construction. Industries which could not run on digital platforms were affected badly, caused shut down of many industries. There was immediate drop in income levels due to unemployment and per capita income was affected. Businesses which could go digital such as e-learning, essential services like food and grocery delivery services, telecommunication services became important to run our lives. It extensively affected financial condition of communities because of disintegration of economy.

Pandemic impacted our living style, health, employment and education. There was helplessness with restriction on movement due to lockdown. Children with no schooling came as another challenge which several amongst us experienced. Closure of educational institutes, schools and colleges had a huge impact on education. Unemployment, salary cuts and children's education were some worries which affected several amongst us. Home isolation if suspected with mild symptom of corona virus was really threatening. It was extremely difficult to face the challenges, although it was a critical time for career growth but Pandemic impacted job prospects of several professionals.

CHAPTER II

Coping with new normal

Technological advancements rapidly took over everything and assured Government, Industries, business services, schools, hospitals and health care services not affected. Digitalization paced up everything in difficult times, where technological breakthroughs like virtual Reality, Augmented Reality, Google Al were significantly used for performance improvement across varied sectors.

Technological breakthroughs like wrist-wearable device to track patients, Telco's using caller tunes, bulk messages and notifications to spread awareness about corona virus were quite helpful for communities. There was rapid increase in healthcare services to support infected patients.

People made sincere efforts and settled down with a new routine which prompted several to alter their homes to adjust with remote working options. Technology helped in normal working of our jobs, education and was significant in coping with new normal. Online schooling and remote working were accelerated during lockdown. Technology made our lives easier and speed up community development in the time of crisis hence emerged as a powerful tool in recovering from the impact of Pandemic.

CHAPTER III

Effect of digitalization on way of working

Pandemic drastically affected the productivity of businesses and health of teams became a severe concern of organizations. Organizations could set up a new culture of remote working and run businesses through digital platforms and could reduce the administrative cost by working remotely. It affected several Professionals to think differently which enhanced capability development and motivated people to adapt to a new culture of remote working and revolutionized lives of several Professionals.

Remote working increased the demand for technology like faster internet and videoconferencing apps. We should be grateful to organizations for facilitating us with Products and services. Digitalization transformed our way of working which prompted several Professionals to develop new skills and gain knowledge about technological aids. Nationwide lockdown confined us to our homes but technology was significant in keeping our work functional. Remote working facilitated several Professionals by providing flexibility and increased productivity along with better work life balance.

Pandemic affected the world technologically, those with access to internet and those without internet access and their livelihood. Pandemic had a great impact on workforcethus affected several Industries with little or no work force available. Industries which were thriving once had substantially gone down. Unemployment, salary cuts and even layoffs were seen amongst Professionals which caused mental stress and trauma. Businesses, ventures and firms which could not go digital suffered.

CHAPTER IV

Remote working affected leadership styles

With online mode of working, it was difficult to streamline teams and team building became difficult. In addition to this, some of the challenges which were being faced while working remotely such as Technology hiccups like no internet connection, video conferencing apps were not always reliable but still most of the organizations preferred remote working. Other times, it was difficult to motivate people to work which affected work efficiency. Sometimes enthusiasm and zeal was missing which was difficult for leaders to work on but despite several hurdles organizations could set up an ecosystem which encouraged profitability. Pandemic changed perspective of several Professionals towards recognizing, understanding, analyzing and rectifying problems more wisely. It was struggling to deal with video-conferencing apps, messages, notifications and social networking. Job insecurity across levels prompted several to adapt skills like resilience which contributed to better Management of people around. Remote working developed a culture of learning and development which helped several Professionals to be more innovative and proved vital for several startups.

Working remotely helped in focusing, creative thinking and greater productivity. A comfortable environment at home helped generating new ideas and thoughts. Remote working affected individual accountability and teams started taking initiatives to be more creative which gained trust of leaders and timely completion of work improved team cohesion. Several products were launched related to healthcare, wellbeing, online education. Looking at the current situations, Creativity is not just an opportunity but responsibility of every conscious individual. Creativity and innovation is essential for accelerating the scale of economies.

CHAPTER V

Era of unicorn companies

Pandemic hit the world equally but people responded differently. It's always easy to crib about the situation but a courageous task to overcome difficult situations. It prompted startup, firms and ventures to think differently and prompted business leaders to re-align strategies and aim towards innovation for maximum revenue generation. There was exponential growth in Ed-tech, online gaming, Agri-tech, Healthcare and online marketing. Despite of crisis, these sectors boom during recent times and became fastest growing sectors which created employment opportunities for several Professionals. Venture capitalists who invested in emerging organizations could witness growth and was beneficial for several startups. Demographers, policy makers and authorities supported by providing easy loans and contributed to capital expenditure.

In addition to this, thrust on innovation and continuous development helped organizations to thrive but yet there are gaps and organizations need to work on Business values and ethics which is only possible by minimizing employee layoffs which is emerging rapidly across industries. It's important to work on effective resource planning and manpower utilization to enhance productivity and incorporate big picture to people for making an organization a Brand which is only possible by igniting Passion and commitment towards work.

Organizations need to revamp strategies in order to increase brand equity in marketplace and reach epitome of success, to be a Decacorn which may be a next milestone for aspiring entrepreneurs.

CHAPTER VI

Remote working and workholism

A commonly used word these days, Work from Home or work remotely is a flexibility to plan both work and home life. We can plan our day and start working as early as possible. It offers a better work/life balance and ease provided by organizations to work from anywhere. It is a step forward to sustainable living because it's saving cost like commutation expense, maintenance of vehicle and moreover contributing to practices like less air and noise pollution which are sustainable towards environment. It is a way forward to environmental sustainability.

There is less stress and one can work at own pace and environment which can be relaxing and leads to better productivity. Although, remote working helped Professionals in multifarious ways like improved performance, less commutation stress, saving money and time, less office politics but at the same, it's enhancing workholism amongst professionals particularly at leadership and strategic levels because of implementation of revenue generating strategies. There is significant rise in workholism, this may be due to strong inner drive to excel. Teams with revenue generating streams are much affected which are indeed contributing to organizational growth and profits. On the other hand, amongst some it has increased innovation and creativity as compared to their counterparts which increased competitive advantage.

CHAPTER VII

Pandemic affected monopolistic markets

Pandemic impacted the industry worldwide but certain industries like Information & communication Technology sector could survive during Pandemic. Adoption of software applications and Software as a service proved vital for organizations which slow down the impact of coronavirus on Industries and contributed to digital economy. It gave opportunity to organizations to preserve revenue streams during Pandemic. Excessive usage of digitalization to support e-learning, online education and remote working was advantageous for industries in bringing good results and increase the market share of Industry.

Pandemic affected consumer behaviour. For an instance, usage of e-commerce sites has increased with time. In addition to this, telecommunication has become an essential service in order to follow the social distancing norm which is subsequently accelerating the need for better internet connectivity. WiFi and internet connectivity is a fundamental need and it's no more a luxury. Sometimes, poor network performance affects the work because mobile data traffic has increased and internet connectivity is a real challenge which hampers the work. It will be worth to mention how Internet Service Providers meet this challenge of providing better network in coming years. There is rapid increase in the usage of internet which has prompted organizations to come up with innovative products to facilitate the current demand which affected monopolistic market with greater financial liquidity. For an instance, adhering to the social distancing norms and consumer had no other option but to purchase online and make digital payments which saved people from infection. Pandemic boosted monopolization which became a growing market for several products. There was growing demand of products related to health care and well being which created a cut-throat competition amongst organizations. Some successful products could generate steady revenues. Pandemic has been a learning experience for entrepreneurs. Social distancing norms and remote work prompted several professionals to go creative in order to meet the evolving consumer needs. Every business is going digital which is creating a demand for different products in the marketplace but there are several niche markets in the digital workplace which are yet to be explored.

CHAPTER VIII

India's response to Pandemic – Aatmanirbhar

Aatmanirbhar Bharat – Initiative of Government to be self sufficient became a driving force amongst youngsters to achieve and revive efficiency amongst communities. This initiative contributed to industries like manufacturing, craftsman goods, cottage industry and artisans which contributed to the growth of small medium enterprise. It gave employment opportunities to several labourers and wagers.

Unemployment due to restructuring of organizations and lack of stable jobs prompted several professionals to adapt to digital platforms which encouraged careers like consulting, blogging, personal training, clothing, designing, manufacturing, health care and food services. Better career prospects in Publishing, creative writing, manuscript writing, journal writing, audio books, podcast, bloggers, editing & proof reading captured several professionals to explore various growth opportunities and to work towards strengthening abilities with changing times. Identify passion which creates a sense of empowerment and benevolence in today's generation. With the hustle bustle of life, Professionals who never got time to reinvent careers but got an opportunity to make a career choice by working on a skill set. Online courses with lucrative offers were in demand. Courses offered comprehensive knowledge in respective fields and plethora of information on internet helped people to grab opportunities. Learning and development programmes helped professionals to grow and helped Millennial in building promising careers. It provided entrepreneurial edge to professionals and they could think of establishing their own ventures. It's imperative to understand the significance of self –reliance for today's generation.

CHAPTER IX

Realization of goals and Self efficacy

We often gauge our lives with good or bad experiences; keep on measuring them time to time. We feel happy on our achievements but feel shattered when we encounter something bad but it's commonly said that whatever happens, happens for good. Some people accept this fact happily and try to align themselves with the unpleasant change, some resist change. Have we ever thought what makes us not to change ourselves and be in the same comfort zone because we are not aware about the cycles of success and failure? There are cycles of success and cycles of failure. Failure happens when we resist change. When everything goes disintegrated and we enter into the vicious cycle, when we do not go with the flow of life, we often suffer. We seldom change ourselves but change is inevitable part of our lives and is important for our growth and success.

On the contrary, cycle of success begins when we start believing in our own capabilities which we often overlook. It's only possible when we get connected to our core values and the foremost is to be honest towards our aspirations but in today's transient world is it possible to live our aspirations when we are loaded with ample of responsibilities and find difficulty in understanding myriad intricacies of life and hardly get time to focus on our aspirations in life, but it's commonly said that where there is a will, there is a way. Self motivation is a key to meet goals which gives confidence to drive our own self.

Pandemic proved as a catalyst for change and transformed us in numerous ways. Pandemic gave us time to rethink about - our goal pursuits and self efficacy beliefs. We started looking at life from different perspective and we could find ways to live a purposeful life which redirected several Professionals towards higher goals. When we move towards higher goals we are more aligned with vision for success. Self reliance or working hard to earn our own success is a key to happiness which can drive several Professionals to achieve more, but in order to achieve one has to connect with the core values like creativity, knowledge, learning and wisdom. Inner wisdom and creativity which we all are blessed with can guide us to overcome difficult situations. It can enhance not just our life but lives of people who are around us and we can find ourselves living a harmonious life.

But why do we fail to reach our goals because we often lose focus or simply give up. The best way to stay focused is to work on Intellectual wellness which involves challenging our abilities, critical thinking and most important is to value our own skills. Strengthen our intellectual abilities at every juncture of life by expanding the horizon of knowledge through study development. It will enhance intellectual Self-confidence which gives strength to manage whatever comes our way.

Therefore, we should not leave any opportunity to acquire a new skill. It's commonly said that learning is a continuous process – we learn through various modes in life but a change happens when we are receptive to learn something new. Instead of cribbing about the situation, it's good to face with courage because it might open a gateway to a new opportunity. Solving the most difficult situations in life with confidence by adopting the intellectual traits like integrity, perseverance, courage, humbleness and fair mindedness. It may help gaining success, happiness and growth.

Why it's important to live for a purpose. When we start living for a purpose we are open to other perspectives of growth. Each day brings new learning's and we must strive to learn something new then only we can find our self aligned with people who are progressive and visionary. It's a purpose which determines the direction we take in our life. It affects our decisions, choices and course of action which defines our future and is a foundation of better tomorrow. It's important to establish a vision for success which can only be facilitated by setting aims and objectives but only a few people are able to achieve their goals and set higher goals in one's life. The first and foremost is to make ourselves aware about goals. It's good to break it down into short term goals which can make it easier and achievable. For that self motivation is the key and wisdom to pave the way. Knowledge is the foundation of development but wisdom is a true knowledge.

CHAPTER X

A value system for Professional survival

Remote working is a preferred mode which is arising amongst professionals, there is ease of working but Work from home doesn't mean just to login zoom App. It's important for organizations to create a system which is important for survival if something uncertain happens in future. To survive in the race, it's important to work on terminal and instrumental values. Terminal values are aims/objectives which we set in life. Instrumental values are the preferable modes of behavior or means to achieve terminal values.

Leadership skills –It's significant for organizations to adapt a strategy which contributes to achieve excellence through people but it's difficult to combine teams when they are working remotely. A strong leadership can save to get through tough times.

Time Management- Significance of Time Management is capturing minds of professionals which may contribute to less stress for successful accomplishment of goals.It's essential to manage time wisely. It's important to stay organized, prepare a to-do list and leave procrastination despite being at home. Timely completion of work is also a skill.

Effective communication – Communication plays a significant role in making our lives successful. Communication is a key to success. We feel confident in a peer group if we communicate well irrespective of any language. We can overcome linguistic barriers by using right words which are persuasive and we often overlook.

Attitude – A discerning belief, Attitude is everything. It's easy to make an excuse for non-performance like no internet connection or health issue of any family member but it's our attitude which helps in aligning with assigned task during turbulent times.

CHAPTER XI

Effect of digitalization on education

There was revolution amongst several sectors but education became a booming one where demand for remote teaching and learning applications increased due to closure of schools and educational institutes. A substantial increase was seen in virtual learning platforms which kept the learning intact. Educators and School authorities could run schools with the help of e-learning platforms. Extensive Technological Products including live classroom for schools, docs, sheets, and access to emails, explanatory videos, worksheets and interactive sessions with teachers and educators helped students in several ways. Schools were closed and technology proved vital in reviving education. In the absence of schools, implementation of e-learning platforms emerged as a tool and there was a revolution amongst schools to go on digital platforms which required training of teachers and educators to understand online pedagogy courses.

-Effect on Parenting:

During these tough times, everyone's working was different and so parenting towards childcare. Several families had been affected due to nationwide lockdown and not every child got a learning infrastructure, a laptop or a smart phone to support online education. Some children had a good support from parents in doing assignments or supporting e-learning programmes while others might have to face problems due to parental working and no guidance.

In addition to this, Unfamiliarity with using online classroom and tools like usage of Google suite or zoom was initially an exercise to learn. On the other hand, converting casual home environment into the look of the classroom was hectic, along with those managing family interruptions while working was extremely difficult. It was juggling for Professionals to manage their own work along with completion of various assignments and quizzes that were also added in the task list. Proper diet and nutrition, proper hygiene conditions were the key factors which caused fatigue and stress. While some parents had to face income losses and gave a halt to even basic necessities and amenities. Pandemic caused high rate of unemployment even amongst developed societies which further affected family dynamics. It led to work interruptions and financial vulnerability which subsequently caused conflicts and anger prevailed due to several reasons. It affected various sections in a social circle and society at large.

Requisition of e-learning platform

Technology has become integral part of our lives and education is not possible without internet connection and laptop or Smartphone/tablet. Digitalization is a significant factor in today's time to run schools, colleges, institutes or universities.

We should be thankful to organizations for providing e-learning platforms but online education is a self learning tool which requires discipline and is the only determining factor which can make it affective. A complete access to expensive digital learning resources require a laptop or desktop, just a Smartphone is not sufficient for curriculum based learning which is a tool to assess basic academic areas like mathematics, science, language, general knowledge to facilitate elementary education. To have a full access of online assignments, teaching aids and instructional material there is a need of desktop or laptop. Virtual classrooms are more collaborative because it's interactive, and students are actively participating in learning activities. Teacher is more like a guide which is making the learning more effective. Regular usage of assessments through Google form and teachers are constantly sending feedbacks, and sharing with parents via emails. E- Learning is effective because it enables to use related presentation or videos, sharing the screen and web browser tabs which is enhanced learning and is more student centric. During recent times, learning is driven by using mobile apps, for instance, there are several apps which are facilitating learning like a new language, spelling & grammar, puzzles and reading stories. Mobile apps are making the information easily available.

Adapting technology to facilitate learning, teachers had to go through rigorous learning modules for effective implementation of e-learning programmes, preparing online quizzes and assignments. For effective learning experience, high speed internet is required but several students had been affected due to lack of Infrastructure. Families with limited resources had been affected tremendously. Some were borrowing mobile phones and sometimes miss the details being sent by teachers. e-Learning affected students' life and Parents could see their performance in the class. Instructions by parents to take initiative in the class sometimes added woes to students' life.

Online education is not just the responsibility of teachers but role of parents can be exemplary in making it effective by providing a learning environment at home. Online schooling and exam patterns have changed student's life. It's important to educate children about communicating well in online classes, to be precise and ask only relevant questions.

In addition to this, internet is an open source hence it's important to guide children about the optimum use of technology. At the same time, security systems need to ensure the optimum use of technology because excessive digitalization may lead to cybercrime which can be detrimental and may causeserious repercussions. To facilitate this, we need to strengthen Human values and make optimum use of technology for the betterment of society.

Academic Procrastination:

Technology proved vital in reviving education but at the same time had a huge impact on academic procrastination due to postponing of exams and no structured tool to assess online exams. Online schooling significantly affected student's behavior towards study which can be detrimental in years to come. Less human interaction amidst crisis had significantly affected social skills amongst children such as communication with other students had significantly declined. In addition to this, online classes affected students – teacher interaction and students got less time to think and speak. Sports and curricular activities had also been affected.

With more exposure to online classes screen time increased, binge watching and access to online games increased and affected student's physical and mental well being. Online schooling affected student's lifestyle like indiscipline in eating habits and sleeping patterns. They were more prone to sedentary lifestyle, easy going or laid back approach than to be disciplined in virtual classes. Online schooling disrupted the routine of waking up on time and no particular time for meals.

Online classes affected well being-

Online schooling and use of technology for various purposes caused several health issues. Usage of gadgets, smart Phones for online classes became a trend which significantly increased the mobile exposure and was challenging for parents to tackle. Communities were apprehensive about the long term impact of smart phones because of its detrimental effect on well being which most of us realized during lockdown and some experienced ill-effects like procrastination and sedentary lifestyle with no or less physical activity. Awe-aspiring audios and videos, gaming apps fascinated children for longer hours which unknowingly affected the cognitive abilities and attention span. Attention span is the amount of time spent to concentrate on a particular task which is essential but has substantially declined over years. Meditation can help in increasing attention span amongst children.

Effect on Teaching/ Non-Teaching Professionals

A great respect for teachers who had been mentoring children via virtual platforms. Teachers worked hard to cope with the changing teaching styles. Conducting webinars and interacting with students, listening to the queries of parents and maintaining discipline in online classes was tough for teachers.

Income level of non-academic staff affected due to closure of schools. There was huge lose to several small vendors who were relying on school institutions like books, stationary or uniform Shops and had to bear a loss. Apart from non-academics, other activities like outdoor sports had significantly been affected. Several libraries and book stores were closed due to closure of school, colleges and universities.

Education at wider scale:

Parents always endeavor for better education and well being of children. Have we ever thought how we can contribute as a parent not just by showing our concern but being agile in our actions?

Spending time in cleanliness, fitness, music and art, pet care and volunteering in social activities is least supported and it gives us more happiness if a child spends more time in improving academics. Creativity is equally important as logical ability because it helps in implementing new ideas, thoughts. It's commonly said that imagination is more important than knowledge because it gives us wisdom to apply our knowledge but factors which crush the creativity amongst children is our habit of saying no to their thoughts and focus more on grades.

At the same time, Isn't it a time to see learning at a wider scale and introduce new concepts of learning in a child's life? With rising expectations of parents and competition in all aspects of life, sometimes happiness is robbed but we have to compete in order to survive in this constantly changing world and education is no more an exception.

Why do we often rely too much on schools, teachers and exaggerate ourselves to be taught in schools. Although, some important skills can easily be taught at home and can help children in aligning with academic goals. To facilitate above, we just need to alter our own lifestyle. We can help them teaching these skills at home only but demands continuous monitoring and discipline by parents for desirable outcomes.

Anger Management: The most significant is Self Management and self control which is the most essential in achieving goals in life. Children get anxious very easily. We focus more on grades than self control and self awareness which affects child's ability to learn. Is it sufficient to work only on Cognition (IQ)? Gone are the days, when intelligence was measured only by IQ but role of Imagination (EQ) is also essential. For an instance, it is commonly witnessed that some children despite of having above-average IQ often found impulsive. Although they are highly intellectual but are at greater risk towards the problems. On the contrary, there are children with average IQ live more successful lives later on. Have we ever tried to rectify this problem? But before that It is utmost important to know the factors determining high or low EQ (imagination) which affects a child's life. It's extremely important to provide healthy environment at home to facilitate effective learning. It's most useful and facilitates positive parenting especially when we are going through challenging times. Being polite, kind and nice with your child means you are respecting his/her opinions or thoughts, on the contrary if we do not give attention to child's opinion it can break the bridge which can be detrimental. Although, it's difficult to stay calm and cool but practice. Politeness is a behavior which can negate the effect of negativity or rudeness. Keep few minutes of your day reserve for your child. It's another important habit which needs to be developed for strong emotional bond with your child. This is not a lot but it is sufficient to balance a child's need. Looking at a piece of art made by your child or a poem or a jingle sang by your child can bring a smile on your child's face which is irreplaceable. Listen to your child carefully no matter even if it is frivolous is a good practice.

Empathy: It's an ability to feel what others are feeling. It must be developed amongst young children because it can help them align with teachers, educators and other children.

Develop a hobby: Developing a productive hobby can make your child's life happier. In simple words, it's a way to channelize energy.

Ethical learning: Along with grades, children need to be developed intellectually and morally. It's important to enhance cognitive abilities where they can learn from their own experiences and surroundings. With changing times, it's getting difficult but we still have to develop them.

CHAPTER XII

Pandemic synergize Indian value system

During nationwide lockdown, we learnt to manage with existing resources which came out as another experience for all of us and we learnt to survive with little. Several faced multifarious issues such as health and finance, education, savings and investmentbut it could only be possible during lockdown that we could spend time at home.

Pandemic synergize Indian value system. We consistently work hard for our families and children to improve quality of life but have we ever thought what is the most important factor which determines happiness of our families and children other than material gains – it's our precious time.

Pandemic provided a wonderful opportunity to spend quality time with children. With a hustle bustle of life, the family time was just restricted but countrywide lockdown provided an opportunity and created memories which we will cherish for long. Hilarious jokes made the environment jovial which we never thought can be more rewarding. Children could enjoy parental love which today's generation was deprived of due to hectic work schedules. Sharing regular family meals and household chores brought everyone together. Another trend which was really enjoyed during lockdown was classic Indian TV shows and trend of board games vanished the fear of corona virus.

Starting a day with a kitchen full of utensils and household chores. Communities were under home quarantine with no option but to cook regular meals at home and at the same time managing our jobs, household chores - An exhausting routine which most of us experienced during lockdown but it's perfectly fine if we were stressed and anxious because we are humans, not robots.

In addition to this, closure of food outlets and restaurants prompted several amongst us to cook at home. Supplying regular meals, household chores and cleanliness though was exhausting but gave amazing mental strength. Incredible stamina to work continuously. Now we can say, we can do multitasking.

Children felt more relaxed with our presence. We could find interests/hobbies in our children that can be nurtured in years to come which are necessary for imparting happiness. Lockdown was tough but we could find ample space in children's lives by assisting them in studies and becoming their teacher, guide, friend and a companion.

Fear of infection prompted us to explore different herbs in our routine. Homemade kadha made up of herbs which most of us preferred for sore throat or fever. Though proved a remedy against infection. Awareness about herbal products for boosting immunity proved preventive. Pandemic taught us everything about good health which created awareness about ayurveda, ancient science and have been curing several diseases from centuries and increased inquisitiveness amongst young generation to know more about it, a legacy to today's generation but we need to reinvent it and there is wider scope of growth for younger generation to learn about it.

Most of us missed morning walk and visiting lush green gardens was prohibited by authorities. At this time, yoga/ meditation saved our lives, to energize our self and beat the day long challenges. A calm and tranquil environment at home benefited our mental and physical well being. At the same time, awareness about balanced diet could help us keeping fit and healthy.

Nationwide lockdown brought different challenges; though most of us volunteered do domestic work which created a humor at the same time connected us to our core values. Cleanliness is our core value. For instance, staying organized in our day to day life helps us to focus. On the contrary unorganized, filthy and dirt like areas make us incoherent. Why is it important to stay organize, the foremost reason is to reduce stress which often occurs with messy surroundings. It's extremely important to put things at assigned places. Failing such habits, may create a chaos or rage at home but can be corrected.

It's important for young generation to understand the significance of sustainable living. It's important to cultivate certain habits in early stages of life because if not corrected will turn into a behavior once they grow up. They will never learn the importance of cleanliness. Parents have been successful in teaching their children about the significance of cleanliness for better quality of life and encouraging sustainable living. Likewise, authorities have been successful in spreading awareness about cleanliness but we are still the half way. It's extremely important to teach our children about environmental sustainability. Awareness about environment degradation is important for young generation to understand and practices towards sustainable living can save the environment from disaster like save electricity and leave less carbon footprints, prefer walk, concept of rain water harvest.

Effect on social lives

Social activities were curtailed and closure of malls, shopping centers, and multiplexes to control the spread of virus affected us enormously. Content streaming services like Netflix and Amazon Prime helped people to cope with challenges #stay home, stay safe which increased usage of internet in our lives. Pandemic affected today's generation in different ways but technological advancements helped people in staying at home. Several mobile apps related to health care, studies, news, fitness and online buying facilitated to deal with everyday challenges.

CHAPTER XIII

Impact of Pandemic on internet usage

Some common hash tags # stay home stay safe, # wash hands, # wear a mask, #social distancing during countrywide lockdown. Demand for internet services was increased during lockdown but proved vital for communities. Nationwide lockdown separated family members and people felt stuck up. Flights, trains and buses were not operating normally and there was anxiety amongst people who were far away from their families due to several reasons. Our older generation was vulnerable during Pandemic but embraced the technology wisely and learnt skills which not only saved them from infection but to live a dignified life. Adhering to the social distancing norms, digital payments were accelerated to avoid the health risk. Digital wallets were secure and convenient which facilitated financial transactions without any hassle. Online purchasing was more preferred. Adhering to the social distancing norms, digital payments were encouraged to reduce the risk of contamination. Instant money transfer apps provided ease to move through tough times.

During home quarantine, expert speakers, practitioners and doctors who shared videos to help the patients were effective. Motivational speakers and TED-ex talks helped several professionals to boost the moralewho were in home isolation due to coronavirus symptoms. Another trend which gained popularity amongst children although provided a source of income, information to several professionals during turbulent times. Various YouTube channels related to healthcare, wellbeing, music, comedy and monetization by digital sources was commonly seen amongst communities. However, created a workplace to earn being at home.

CHAPTER XIV

Changing lifestyle

One of the important measures during lockdown was to stay at home which prompted several amongst to renovate our homes and made it comfy to adjust with a set up of online classes and remote working. During lockdown, we could think of renovating and change the décor of our homes but to buy anything new was challenging because leaving our homes was prohibited and we could tweak to give a new look to our home. All this happened because we could spend time at home.

Although it was hectic but household chores helped in balancing screen time which turned out to be a learning opportunity for all of us. We learnt to be more disciplined in terms of our well being. More precisely to stay in the race of survivors and saved ourselves from corona virus it was essential. We could understand about aesthetic value of food which was evading but replenished during recent times and proved therapeutic in fighting against infection. A balanced diet is significant in rejuvenating our mind, body and soul.

At the same time, it's extremely important to refrain from gadgets for few minutes of the day which ensures physical and mental well being. Yoga or meditation can be helpful in dealing with stress. Focus on meditation and suitable physical exercise is also important for the smooth functioning of our body but yes with changing times, human interaction has been affected and we are social beings. It's important to socialize for our happiness and well being because technology may destroy human interaction in years to come.

CHAPTER XV

Pandemic lessons

It was tough time for all of us but it's commonly said that best lessons of life are learnt during tough times. A life disruption disease which affected every aspect of our lives. It caused significant damage to humanity and shattered our lives. Life is uncertain and we never thought that our lives will suddenly be affected due to coronavirus but despite the fact we could get up and walk, hope that our lives will be normal. This crisis tested our abilities and how do we survive in this ever changing world. It's commonly said that hope sustains life. Can we relate hope to probability? Hope keeps probability alive. It was only the hope which could ameliorate the situation and several could survive during crisis. This is the basis of our existence and that's how we are evolved as a species. Nothing is permanent in this world. With the passage of time, everything will be fine but important is what lessons we learnt from this situation. A greatest lesson that Pandemic taught us that our life is precious. True happiness can only be found in being grounded. It's not a time to be lenient although what we need today is compassion, empathy and generosity instead of hatred and violence. Cherish happy moments. Celebrate life and live the moment. There are people who leave their homes to earn their living and some are dependent on other people's help for feeding themselves or government hence, we should feel blessed if we can stay at home and we are sheltered with enough resources to keep us safe from the infection. Every moment of life is unique and significant in its own way. It's up to us how do we utilize it – we exhaust the day achieving nothing substantial or improve each day by adding value to it. At the same time taking good care of our health and keep ourselves updated about the health care campaigns run by government is also important. Human aspirations become futile in the absence of good health which is an important factor to be taken care in today's time. To stay focused towards our goals, we need to pay attention towards our health first. Good health enables to carry out admirable deeds which are much needed in today's time. The fundamental theory of motivation has also been affected and now safety needs have become everyone's priority. We can achieve our goals only when we are alive, life is uncertain.

CHAPTER XVI

When Pandemic will end

No one in the world can predict when Pandemic will be over but danger is still looming around us and we should be thankful to government, scientists, health care Professionals for providing vaccines and saving our lives. Successful vaccination drives protected people who were vulnerable to the disease which could develop herd immunity but we should still move cautiously such as practices like maintaining proper hygiene, wearing a mask, washing hands regularly should be continued to save from coronavirus.

CHAPTER XVII

For Pro readers

Over years, Internet has revolutionized our lives and enriched us by providing the information at our fingertips. Modern technology created amazing tools like Smartphone, tablets and computers which are portable and has made our lives easier and better. Digital transformation – A term facilitating during recent times and providing competitive edge to several professionals where importance is given to proactive acquisition of technology and tools which allows focusing on creativity and innovation. Pandemic has drastically affected the global economy and the most challenging is to revive the economy by facilitating innovative and creative ideas which is the fundamental need of industries and implement revenue generating strategies. It's a time to head off towards inclusive societies where no one is discriminated on the basis of age, caste, creed, culture or gender but Problem solving skills and development matters the most.

Modern Technology helped communities to connect during Pandemic. We could see the time when technology superseded and a new era of digital learning transformed the educational ecosystem. Authorities could run schools, educational institutes with the help of technological aids, offered e-learning platforms to students which kept the learning intact during lockdown. Schools came out with idea of e-learning in the time of crisis. Explanatory videos, worksheets and interactive sessions with teachers and educators benefited students in several ways. Online schooling helped in setting up a routine and school work assignments kept children active lockdown. E-learning platforms were highly beneficial but it affected certain skills. Schools not only benefited students in academics but in other skills too which significantly contributed to the holistic development of a student like self awareness, discipline, interaction in a peer group, and communication. Such learning's are abstract which was not possible in e-learning platforms but e-learning was the only way out than no learning at all.

Role of technology was significant in transforming communities to digital platform which brought a quantum shift at Industry level in response to pandemic situation. However, certain communities were not able to avail basic amenities. Pandemic impacted educational system because schools were completely closed and several students who left without education because they had no access to online education. People who were struggling for physiological needs like water, electricity, food and shelter. Geographical restrictions, low literacy rate and income levels affected the digital growth. Lack of proper infrastructure and connectivity drastically affected studies and employment opportunities. Closure of schools immensely impacted education and affected several students. To meet the current demand of online education, Computer literacy and facilities like smart phones, laptops amongst underprivileged sections of society is essential. They are not just deprived of smart phones but are not intellectual enough to guide their children. Government need to strengthen the remote learning for underprivileged sections also and caring for destitute should also be in the to-do list because education is a fundamental right of every child. Similarly, digital literacy programmes should be supported in order to educate people about the remote learning. Better Internet connectivity is what can connect people and help societies to thrive. Government should look forward to fill these gaps and provide support to rural communities.

In this digital age, technology should be available to everyone because it is a way forward to transformation in sectors like education, health care, skill development and job creation in public services. However, new technologies are sustainable towards environment, saving natural resources and less likely to pollute the environment. Rapid technological advancements are helping to restore the planet.

In today's scenario, where climate change is another cause of worry. Heat waves, floods, landslides, volcanic eruptions, earth quakes and several other natural disasters have shaken the world. When Non-renewable energy resources are depleting and awareness about energy resources is essential. We are facing the most threatening existential challenges but we can win over the crisis when we are together irrespective of any caste, creed, religion or culture. Young generation have a great responsibility to ensure that the world becomes a more peaceful place but it's only possible if we emphasis on compassion, empathy and generosity, focus more on sustainable living rather than hatred and violence to beat the upcoming challenges.

Bibliography

https://www.ventureintelligence.com/Indian-Unicorn-Tracker.php

https://www.globenewswire.com/news-release/2022/03/01/2394038/28124/en/Global-E-Learning-Market-2022-to-2027-Industry-Trends-Share-Size-Growth-Opportunity-and-Forecasts.html

https://en.unesco.org/news/unesco-figures-show-two-thirds-academic-year-lost-average-worldwide-due-Pandemic-school

https://news.un.org/en/story/2021/03/1088812

About The Author

A Master's degree in Business Administration and over ten years of experience in various HR domains like Talent Acquisition & Operations, employee engagement. Her passion to learn new skills embarked her on a journey of an author where she used her writing skills to explain the IMPACT OF PANDEMIC.

As she climbed up the corporate ladder, she was able to gain ample knowledge about IT Industry and varied technological advancements with passing years of her Professional experience. She has used some technical terms to explain the impact of pandemic on digitalization and subsequently on other industries.

Her keen interest to learn Agile HRM which is a growing interest of several HR Professionals and substantial for sustainable growth of organizations.

Printed by Libri Plureos GmbH in Hamburg,
Germany